Where in the World Can I . . .

RIDE
A
CAMEL?

**WORLD
BOOK**

www.worldbook.com

World Book, Inc.
180 North LaSalle Street, Suite 900
Chicago, Illinois 60601
USA

For information about other World Book publications, visit our website at **www.worldbook.com** or call **1-800-WORLDBK (967-5325).**

For information about sales to schools and libraries, call 1-800-975-3250 (United States), or 1-800-837-5365 (Canada).

Library of Congress Cataloging-in-Publication Data for this volume has been applied for.

Where in the World Can I…
ISBN: 978-0-7166-2178-2 (set, hc.)

Ride a Camel?
ISBN: 978-0-7166-2185-0 (hc.)

Also available as:
ISBN: 978-0-7166-2195-9 (e-book)

Printed in China by Shenzhen Wing King Tong Paper Products Co., Ltd., Shenzhen, Guangdong
1st printing July 2018

STAFF

Writer: Grace Guibert

Executive Committee
President
  Jim O'Rourke

Vice President and
Editor in Chief
  Paul A. Kobasa

Vice President, Finance
  Donald D. Keller

Vice President, Marketing
  Jean Lin

Vice President,
International Sales
  Maksim Rutenberg

Vice President, Technology
  Jason Dole

Director, Human Resources
  Bev Ecker

Editorial
Director, New Print
  Tom Evans

Managing Editor, New Print
  Jeff De La Rosa

Senior Editor, New Print
  Shawn Brennan

Editor, New Print
  Grace Guibert

Librarian
  S. Thomas Richardson

Manager, Contracts &
Compliance (Rights &
Permissions)
  Loranne K. Shields

Manager, Indexing Services
  David Pofelski

Digital
Director, Digital Product
Development
  Erika Meller

Manager, Digital Products
  Jonathan Wills

Graphics and Design
Senior Art Director
  Tom Evans

Coordinator, Design
Development and
Production
  Brenda Tropinski

Media Researcher
  Rosalia Bledsoe

**Manufacturing/
Production**
Manufacturing Manager
  Anne Fritzinger

Proofreader
  Nathalie Strassheim

TABLE OF CONTENTS

WHAT IS A CAMEL?

Camels are large, strong animals that live in or around deserts. There are two types of camels.

The Arabian (*uh RAY bee uhn*) camel has one hump on its back. Arabian camels are also called dromedary (*DROM uh DEHR ee*) camels.

The Bactrian *(BAK tree uhn)* camel has two humps.

Here is an easy trick to remember how many humps each type of camel has. Imagine the capital letters *B* and *D* on their sides. B has two humps, like the *Bactrian* camel, and D has one hump, like the *Dromedary* camel!

B

Bactrian

D

Dromedary

Camels like to eat desert plants, grains (oats and wheat, for example), grasses, and fruit. Camels can go for weeks without food. Their humps store fat, which camels' bodies use for energy when food is scarce. When this has been used up, the camels' humps can sag.

8

Camels can also go for days or even months without drinking water. A thirsty camel may drink up to 50 gallons (200 liters) of water in a single day! But camels can get most of the water they need from their food.

Camels are built for life in the desert. Their long, curly eyelashes keep sand out of their eyes. Camels have thick eyebrows that shield their eyes from the hot desert sun.

Camels have small, rounded ears. The ears are covered with hair and sit far back on a camel's head. This protects camels' ears from the blowing sand and dust.

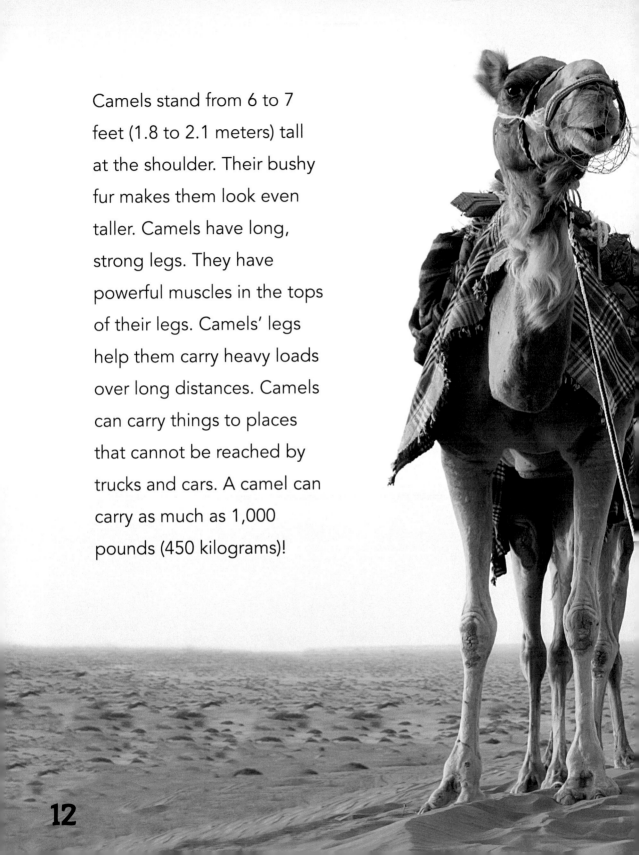

Camels stand from 6 to 7 feet (1.8 to 2.1 meters) tall at the shoulder. Their bushy fur makes them look even taller. Camels have long, strong legs. They have powerful muscles in the tops of their legs. Camels' legs help them carry heavy loads over long distances. Camels can carry things to places that cannot be reached by trucks and cars. A camel can carry as much as 1,000 pounds (450 kilograms)!

The shape of camels' feet allows them to walk easily on the soft sand. Camels have two long toes on each foot. A *hoof* grows at the front of each toe. A hoof is a hard covering on some animals' feet. Cows, horses, and many other animals walk on their hoofs. But camels walk on a *pad* that connects the two toes. A pad is a cushionlike part of an animal's foot. Camels' cushioned feet help them walk across loose sand.

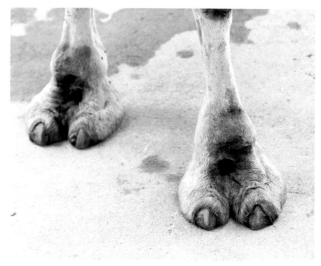

"SHIPS OF THE DESERT"

Camels usually walk, especially in the heat. When they must go faster, camels either gallop or *pace*. The pace is a medium-speed movement in which both legs on the same side lift together and come down together.

This action makes a swaying motion that makes some camel riders "seasick." For this reason, people sometimes call camels "ships of the desert."

Camels are also called "ships of the desert" because they have helped people live in and travel through the desert for thousands of years.

Camels can carry people and heavy loads long distances across the desert sand. They have been very useful to desert-dwelling peoples throughout history. Ancient people showed camels in pottery, sculpture, and other objects the people made.

Camels have even been used in wars and battles. Camel *cavalries (KAV uhl reez)* have been used in desert battles since at least 853 B.C. A cavalry is a unit of soldiers who ride on the backs of animals. Napoleon Bonaparte *(nuh POH lee uhn BOH nuh pahrt)*, a French general, famously used camels in battle in the 1800's.

Today, millions of people still depend on camels to help with everyday tasks. Camels pull plows, transport goods, and provide food, clothing, and shelter. In turn, people help camels survive by giving them water in the desert heat.

Arabian camels live in
the desert areas of India,
the Middle East, Africa,
and Australia.

Bactrian camels live in central Asia, mainly in Mongolia and China.

In many of these areas, people use camels for food as well as transportation. People eat camel meat and drink camel milk. They also make cheese from the milk. Camels' soft, woolly fur can also be woven into warm blankets and clothing.

Camels work hard, but sometimes they are stubborn. They may groan or bawl when they are loaded with too much weight. Camels may even kick and spit when they are angry!

Lots of camels roam wild today. But most are cared for by camel owners or *cameleers (KAM uh LIHRZ)*. Cameleers are camel drivers. They can train their camels to stand and kneel on command when they are young. Camels gradually learn to carry weight and saddles. After years of practice, full-grown camels are ready to carry passengers and heavy loads across the desert.

Would you like to ride a camel? Let's take a look at places around the world where you can!

PYNDAN CAMEL TRACKS

Australia is home to about 1 million camels.
Camels were first brought to Australia
around 1840. People used camels
to help them explore and
settle the continent.
Australia is the only
country that is also a
continent.

Australian camels live in central and western Australia. Camels can travel easily through the Australian outback. The outback is the center part of Australia where few people live. The dry, red, sandy soil of parts of the outback is called *pindan (PIHN dan)*.

You can experience Australia's outback and learn about the importance of camels in Australia's history by taking a camel ride with Pyndan Camel Tracks. The tracks are in the town of Alice Springs, in Australia's Northern Territory. Alice Springs is in the Red Centre, an area known for its beautiful desert landscape.

A camel ride with Pyndan Camel Tracks lets riders see this beautiful desert landscape. Pyndan Camel Tracks offers midday, afternoon, and sunset camel tours.

On each tour, cameleers take visitors across parts of the desert where they can see kangaroos *(KANG guh ROOZ)*, wild dogs called dingoes *(DIHNG gohz)*, wallabies *(WOL uh beez)*, birds, lizards, and other Australian wildlife. Then, the cameleer takes riders up a hill for a beautiful view of the rugged MacDonnell Ranges.

The cameleers at Pyndan Camel Tracks take great care of their herd of camels. They make saddles by hand for each camel. The cameleers hope the people who ride with them will value the nature and beauty of Alice Springs. They also work to preserve and protect the plants and animals that live there.

The people of Alice Springs love to celebrate camels and their history in the region. They even host a funny camel race every year called the Camel Cup.

The race began as a joke between friends. Camels sway and wobble when they run. Some camels do not cooperate—they might not run at all! Watching the camel race became popular over the years.

OTHER CAMEL TREKS

THE SILK ROAD

In ancient times, camel *caravans* carried goods across the dry, harsh regions of an area called the Silk Road. Caravans are groups of people and animals that travel together for safety or a shared purpose.

The Silk Road was a popular
trade route between China
and Europe. Merchants and
traders traveled along this
group of routes. The Silk
Road was used mainly from
the 100's B.C. to the A.D.
1500's.

The Silk Road crossed mountains
and deserts in Central Asia and
the Middle East. It stretched
about 5,000 miles (8,050
kilometers)! Bactrian camels,
native to this part of the world,
were used to carry the heavy
loads.

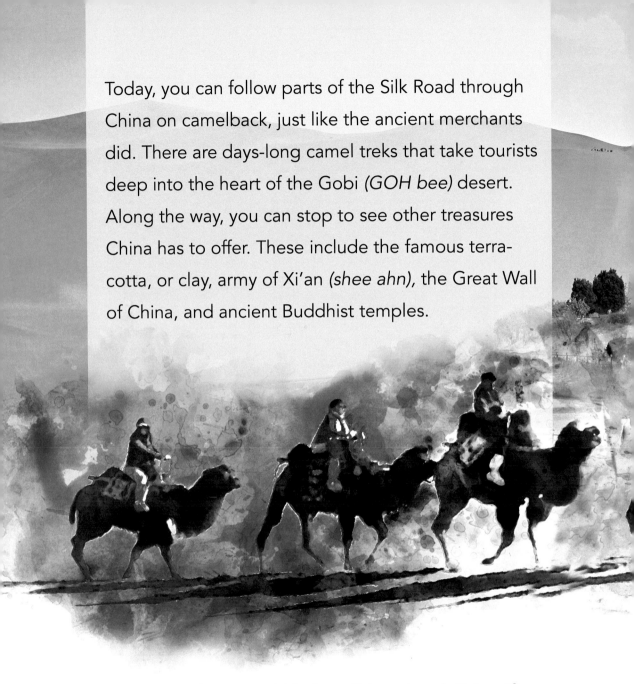

Today, you can follow parts of the Silk Road through China on camelback, just like the ancient merchants did. There are days-long camel treks that take tourists deep into the heart of the Gobi *(GOH bee)* desert. Along the way, you can stop to see other treasures China has to offer. These include the famous terra-cotta, or clay, army of Xi'an *(shee ahn)*, the Great Wall of China, and ancient Buddhist temples.

In 2014, the United Nations Educational, Scientific and Cultural Organization (UNESCO) added places along the Silk Road to its list of World Heritage Sites.

Some World Heritage Sites are special because of the plants and animals that live there. Others are special because of events in history that happened at them. Governments are required to preserve and protect World Heritage Sites.

THE SAHARA

Morocco *(muh ROK oh)* is a country in the northwestern corner of Africa. Much of Morocco is part of the Sahara *(suh HAR uh),* the largest desert in the world.

The land in this desert is harsh. Camels have been used to travel through the Sahara for thousands of years. The people who live in the Sahara are called Berbers *(BUR buhrz).*

Berbers need camels to help them survive in the desert. Many Moroccan Berbers have settled into mountain villages, where they farm and raise animals. Many Berbers still live as *nomads (NOH madz)* in the Sahara. Nomads are people who move from place to place.

A Moroccan camel trek can give travelers a glimpse of Berber life. Camel rides through parts of the Sahara can take you to a Berber camp, where travelers can taste Berber food, listen to traditional Berber music, and enjoy traditional Berber dancing.

The beautiful landscapes, starlit skies, and traditional Berber culture can be an exciting adventure for visitors who wish to get away from Morocco's bustling cities, such as Marrakech *(muh RAH kehsh)*, Fez, and Rabat *(rah BAHT)*.

THE GREAT PYRAMIDS

On the other side of the Sahara desert from Morocco is the Middle Eastern country of Egypt. Since ancient times, people here have used camels to move around the dry, windswept desert land of Egypt. Camels are still used sometimes to move people and heavy loads.

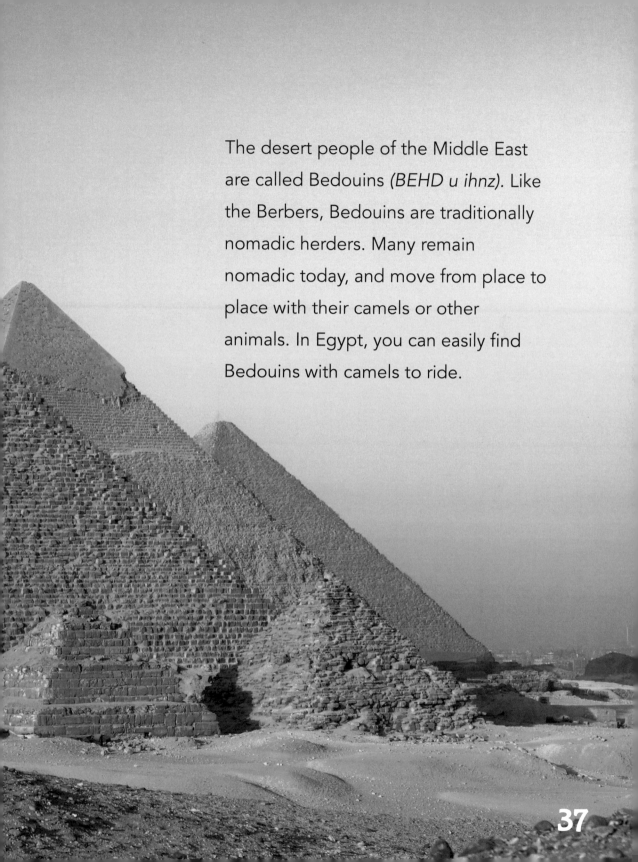

The desert people of the Middle East are called Bedouins *(BEHD u ihnz)*. Like the Berbers, Bedouins are traditionally nomadic herders. Many remain nomadic today, and move from place to place with their camels or other animals. In Egypt, you can easily find Bedouins with camels to ride.

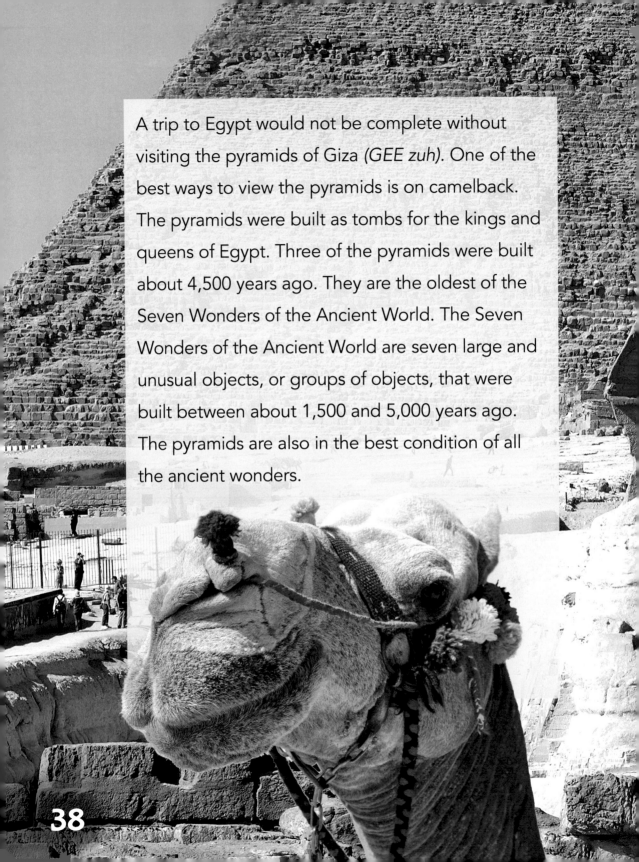

A trip to Egypt would not be complete without visiting the pyramids of Giza *(GEE zuh)*. One of the best ways to view the pyramids is on camelback. The pyramids were built as tombs for the kings and queens of Egypt. Three of the pyramids were built about 4,500 years ago. They are the oldest of the Seven Wonders of the Ancient World. The Seven Wonders of the Ancient World are seven large and unusual objects, or groups of objects, that were built between about 1,500 and 5,000 years ago. The pyramids are also in the best condition of all the ancient wonders.

After you've seen the pyramids, your camel ride can take you to the nearby Great Sphinx (sfihngks). A sphinx is a mythological creature with the head of a human and the body, feet, and tail of a lion. The Great Sphinx honors a king. The monument stretches 240 feet (73 meters) long and stands about 66 feet (20 meters) high. It is carved out of limestone blocks, just like the pyramids. It is also about 4,500 years old.

In 1979, UNESCO made the pyramids of Giza and the Great Sphinx World Heritage Sites.

CAMEL COUSINS

Camels are related to four types of animals that live in South America. Camels are the only animals with humps. But all members of the camel family share other features.

Llamas (*LAH muhz*) measure about 4 feet (1.2 meters) tall at the shoulder when they are fully grown. Like camels, they are useful pack animals and can carry heavy loads. Llamas are the largest South American members of the camel family.

Alpacas *(al PAK uhz)* live in the mountain regions of Bolivia *(boh LIHV ee uh)*, Chile *(CHIHL ee)*, and Peru *(puh ROO)*. Alpacas are a little smaller than llamas. They are usually raised for their soft, warm wool. Their black, white, or brown hair can grow as long as 24 inches (61 centimeters).

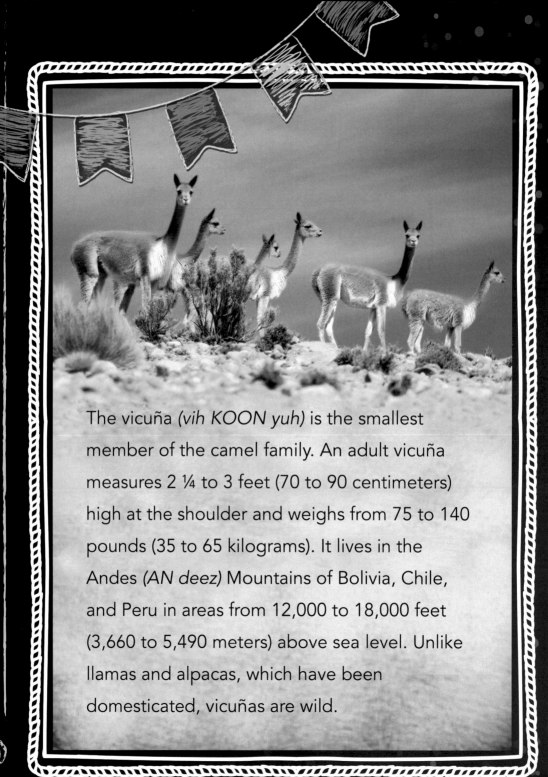

The vicuña *(vih KOON yuh)* is the smallest member of the camel family. An adult vicuña measures 2 ¼ to 3 feet (70 to 90 centimeters) high at the shoulder and weighs from 75 to 140 pounds (35 to 65 kilograms). It lives in the Andes *(AN deez)* Mountains of Bolivia, Chile, and Peru in areas from 12,000 to 18,000 feet (3,660 to 5,490 meters) above sea level. Unlike llamas and alpacas, which have been domesticated, vicuñas are wild.

Guanacos (*gwuh NAH kohz*) are also wild. They live in groups in the foothills of the Andes Mountains in Peru, Chile, and Argentina. Guanacos also live on the Patagonian (*PAT uh GOH nee uhn*) plateau in Argentina. A grown-up guanaco stands 3 ½ to 4 feet (107 to 122 centimeters) high at the shoulder. Guanacos can live in regions that lie up to 14,000 feet (4,300 meters) above sea level.

AT THE ZOO

If you can't make it to the natural desert *habitat* where camels live, you can find camels and their relatives at zoos around the world. A habitat is the place where something lives in the wild. Some zoos may even offer rides on camels, or on llamas, alpacas, or other camel cousins.

Bactrian camels are *critically endangered.* This means that they are in danger of dying out completely. Their habitat and food supply are being threatened, making it hard for them to survive. We must respect and care for endangered animals or they might soon be gone forever.

If you are lucky enough to ride a camel, remember how important camels are to many cultures. A camel ride will be a special experience!

BOOKS AND WEBSITES

BOOKS

Amazing Animals: Camels by Kate Riggs (Creative Education, 2014)
Part of a series on animals and their behavior, this book covers camel basics and includes a folk story explaining how the camel got its hump. It features beautiful photographs.

Camels by Jennifer Zeiger (Scholastic/C. Press/F. Watts Trade, 2015)
This volume of the "Nature's Children" series provides key facts about a camel's life in the desert. The book explains camels' interactions with humans over the years and emphasizes the importance of conservation.

Do You Really Want to Meet a Camel? by Bridget Heos (Amicus Illustrated, 2016)
This book presents information about camels in a narrative nonfiction style. It follows a girl who travels to the Gobi desert and sees a camel. She learns about camels' desert lifestyle.

WEBSITES

National Geographic: Arabian Camel and Bactrian Camel
http://www.nationalgeographic.com/animals/mammals/a/arabian-camel/

http://www.nationalgeographic.com/animals/mammals/b/bactrian-camel/

These websites cover such details as each animal's classification, size, and conservation status. The sites provide an overview of Arabian and Bactrian camels' history, adaptations, and domestication.

National Geographic Kids: Bactrian Camel
http://kids.nationalgeographic.com/animals/bactrian-camel/#camel-humps.jpg

This website provides kid-friendly information with accessible graphics.

Pyndan Camel Tracks
http://www.cameltracks.com/

Provides information about planning a trip to Pyndan Camel Tracks and Australia. Includes biographies of the camels at Pyndan.

INDEX

ACKNOWLEDGMENTS

Cover: © Alberto Loyo, Shutterstock; © ERainbow/
Shutterstock

2-3   © Gigavisual/Dreamstime

5-15   © Shutterstock

16-17   © Bodom/Shutterstock; *Napoleon and His
General Staff* (1867), oil on panel by
Jean-Leon Gerome

18-25   © Shutterstock

26-27   © Historica Graphica Collection/Heritage Images/
Getty Images; © Richard Faragher, Shutterstock

28-29   © Prisma/UIG/Getty Images; © Rudra Narayan
Mitra, Shutterstock

30-31   © Shutterstock

32-33   © Bartosz Hadyniak, iStockphoto;
© Bulent Erdeger, Anadolu Agency/Getty Images

34-35   © Hemis/Alamy Images; © Valentin Armianu,
Dreamstime; © Shutterstock

36-43   © Shutterstock

44-45   © Shutterstock; © Rozenn Leard, Dreamstime